# Built for Speed

# The World's Wildest Roller Coasters

## by Michael Burgan

**Consultant:**
David M. Escalante
Public Relations Director
American Coaster Enthusiasts

## CAPSTONE BOOKS

an imprint of Capstone Press
Mankato, Minnesota

Capstone Books are published by Capstone Press,
1710 Roe Crest Drive, North Mankato, Minnesota 56003.
www.capstonepub.com

*Library of Congress Cataloging-in-Publication Data*
Burgan, Michael.
    The world's wildest roller coasters/by Michael Burgan.
    p. cm.—(Built for speed)
    Includes bibliographical references and index.
    Summary: Describes different kinds of roller coasters, their history and how they
operate, and gives examples of each type.
    ISBN-13: 978-0-7368-0571-1 (hardcover)
    ISBN-10: 0-7368-0571-0 (hardcover)
    ISBN-13: 978-0-7368-8871-4 (softcover pbk.)
    ISBN-10: 0-7368-8871-3 (softcover pbk.)
    1. Roller coasters—Juvenile literature. [1. Roller coasters.] I. Title. II. Built for
speed (Mankato, Minn.)
GV 1860.R64 B87 2001
791'.06'8—dc21                                                   00-021455

**Editorial Credits**
Carrie A. Braulick, editor; Timothy Halldin, cover designer and illustrator; Erin Scott,
    Sarin Creative, illustrator; Katy Kudela, photo researcher

**Photo Credits**
Archive Photos/Nat Norman, 19
Corbis/Andrew J.G. Bell; Eye Ubiquitous, 38 (bottom)
International Stock/Paul Thompson, cover, 22, 25
Isaac Hernández/Mercury Press, 32, 35, 37, 39 (bottom)
Paramount's Kings Dominion, 26, 29, 30, 39 (top)
Paramount's Kings Island, 14, 20, 38 (top), 40
Photo Network/MacDonald Photography, 7
Richard Cummins, 12
Unicorn Stock Photos/Dick Young, 4, 43; Florent Flipper, 10
Visuals Unlimited/John Sohlden, 8

Printed in the United States of America in North Mankato, Minnesota.
052013      007377R

# Table of Contents

# Chapter 1

# Wild Roller Coasters

Amusement parks have many rides. At most amusement parks, roller coasters are the fastest rides. Some coasters travel at speeds of about 100 miles (161 kilometers) per hour. More than 1,000 coasters exist in the world today. More than half of them are in North America.

Roller coasters sometimes are called scream machines. People often scream as they ride coasters. These rides can be thrilling and scary.

## Roller Coasters
The two basic types of coasters are wooden and steel coasters. Beams support a wooden coaster's track. Beams are wooden posts. Piles support a

**People often scream as they ride roller coasters.**

steel coaster's track. Piles are steel posts. Tracks are a series of wooden or metal sections on top of a roller coaster's beams or piles.

Riders sit in cars on most roller coasters. Cars usually are connected to each other to form a small train. Cars often are made of metal coated with plastic. Most cars have seats or benches on which riders sit. Cars also may have shoulder harnesses or lap bars that hold riders in them.

Roller coaster cars have three sets of wheels. The wheels attach to a track's rails. Rails lie on top of tracks. Rails are a pair of steel bars located at the edges of tracks. One set of a car's wheels runs on top of the rails. Another set runs alongside the rails. The third set runs underneath the rails.

Both wooden and steel coasters can be out-and-back or twister coasters. Out-and-back coasters have long, straight tracks with few turns. The tracks form a long oval shape. Tracks on twister coasters wrap over and under themselves. They often have many sharp turns.

**Corkscrews are one type of inversion.**

## Roller Coaster Features
The entire length of a roller coaster's track is called a circuit. A circuit may include inversions, twists, and turns. Any section of a track that causes cars to travel upside down is called an inversion. A loop is one type of inversion. Loops form circular shapes. A corkscrew is another kind of inversion. These sections of tracks twist into spirals.

Centrifugal force is a force related to motion. Centrifugal force pushes objects that are moving in a circle outward. It affects roller coaster riders when cars turn around a curve. Centrifugal force pushes riders to the right when the cars turn left. The force pushes riders to the left when the cars turn right.

Centrifugal force also is present when cars travel on inversions. Centrifugal force must be stronger than gravity as cars travel on inversions. Gravity pulls riders toward the ground. But centrifugal force keeps riders from falling out of their seats. Roller coaster engineers pay close attention to the size and shape of inversions. They make sure inversions will create enough centrifugal force.

# CENTRIFUGAL FORCE

Most roller coaster circuits begin with a lift hill. A chain usually pulls cars up this steep hill. The chain releases the cars at the top of the hill. Gravity then pulls the cars down the hill. This force pulls all objects down toward Earth's surface. Riders often enjoy traveling up and down the lift hill. The cars usually reach their highest speeds near the bottom of this hill. Circuits often have many hills after the lift hill. But the lift hill almost always is the tallest of these hills.

Roller coaster hills have drops. A drop is the section of track cars travel on as they descend hills. Some drops are steep. Others are more level. The slope of a roller coaster's drop is measured in degrees. A flat track has a slope of 0 degrees. A vertical track has a slope of 90 degrees. These tracks are straight up and down.

Brakes lie on roller coaster tracks near stations. Roller coaster rides start and end at stations. A computer operates the brakes for most coasters as the rides end. Amusement park workers operate the brakes on some coasters. The brakes slow the cars down before they enter the station.

The amount of time a roller coaster ride lasts varies. Some rides last less than a minute. Other rides last nearly 4 minutes. The time depends on the length of the coaster's circuit and how fast the cars travel.

## Wooden Coasters

People sometimes call wooden coasters "woodies." Rails on these coasters lie on wooden tracks. The wooden beams move slightly as cars travel along the tracks. This causes woodies to make creaking

noises. The motion and noise can add to the excitement of riding wooden coasters.

Wooden coasters often are difficult to build. Builders must make sure the beams are strong. The beams need to support the tracks and cars. Builders also need to make sure the beams are connected to each other properly.

## Steel Coasters

The world's tallest and fastest roller coasters are made of steel. Rails on these coasters lie on steel tracks. Piles support the tracks. Builders can easily fit the piles together.

Some steel coasters are called "hypercoasters." These coasters have at least one hill that is more than 200 feet (60 meters) high. Hypercoasters often are out-and-back coasters.

Inverted and suspended coasters are other types of steel coasters. Both of these coasters have cars that hang from an overhead track. The cars on inverted coasters are locked in place. Inverted coasters allow riders' legs to hang down from the cars. Many inverted coasters have inversions.

**The world's tallest roller coasters are made of steel.**

**Suspended coasters hang down from an overhead track.**

The cars on suspended coasters swing as they move. Riders' legs are inside the cars.

Suspended coasters do not have inversions. Inversions on these coasters would be dangerous. The coasters' cars could easily tip as they travel on inversions.

Steel coasters also may be bobsled coasters. These coasters have a smooth, rounded steel or fiberglass chute instead of tracks. The wheels of the cars travel along the chute.

Shuttle coasters are another kind of steel roller coaster. The cars on these coasters travel forward and backward over the same section of track. They usually travel up a steep hill at one end of the track. The cars then fall backward down the hill. They travel up another steep hill at the other end of the track. The cars then fall forward to enter the station.

## Indoor and Portable Coasters

Most roller coasters are located at outdoor amusement parks. But some coasters are inside buildings. West Edmonton Mall in Edmonton, Alberta, Canada, has an indoor coaster that is 136 feet (41 meters) high. The Mall of America in Bloomington, Minnesota, has a roller coaster that is 60 feet (18 meters) high. It has 2,680 feet (817 meters) of track.

Some coasters can be regularly moved from one place to another. Workers can easily put together and take apart these coasters. Portable coasters are popular in Europe. Europeans often use these coasters during large celebrations that last several days.

# Chapter 2

# The Beast

The Beast is a wooden roller coaster located at Paramount's Kings Island amusement park. This park is near Cincinnati, Ohio. The Beast is one of the world's most famous wooden coasters. It also is the world's longest wooden coaster. It has 7,400 feet (2,256 meters) of track that covers 35 acres (14 hectares) of the amusement park. The Beast has features of both out-and-back and twister coasters.

At one time, The Beast was the fastest wooden coaster in the world. It remains one of the world's fastest wooden coasters. The Beast has a top speed of 64 miles (103 kilometers) per hour. The world's fastest wooden coaster is Son of Beast. Paramount's Kings Island opened this coaster in

**The Beast travels through a wooded area.**

Gravitational force is measured in units called "g." The g force on a person standing on flat ground is 1 g. Roller coaster riders feel 1 g when a coaster is standing still.

G forces give people weight. G forces of more than 1 make a person heavier. Roller coaster riders feel heavier as a coaster accelerates uphill. Objects gain speed when they accelerate.

G forces of less than 1 make a person lighter. Roller coaster riders feel lighter as a roller coaster accelerates downhill.

Roller coaster riders sometimes feel as if they are weightless during 0 gs. They call this feeling "airtime." Riders often enjoy experiencing airtime during roller coaster rides.

Most roller coasters have g forces of 3.5 or less. High g forces can be dangerous for riders. People can become unconscious at 7 gs. This is because people's blood can rush to their feet during high g forces.. High g forces also can frighten riders. Only a few roller coasters operate at g forces above 6. These are the Mindbender in Canada, the Dreier Looping in England, and the Moonsault Scramble in Japan.

## G Force Effects                                                     Gs

| G Force Effects | Gs |
|---|---|
| Weightlessness | 0 |
| Standing on flat ground | 1 |
| Hands and feet heavy; walking and climbing difficult | 2 |
| Walking and climbing impossible; crawling difficult | 3 |
| Movement only possible with great effort; crawling nearly impossible | 4 |
| Only slight movement of arms and head possible | 5 |

# G FORCES

2000. It has a top speed of 78 miles (126 kilometers) per hour.

## History of Wooden Coasters

Like The Beast, the earliest roller coasters were made of wood. The first roller coasters opened in France during the early 1800s. Early coasters had few steep hills or sharp turns. The cars traveled less than 30 miles (50 kilometers) per hour.

In 1884, the Gravity Pleasure Switchback Railway opened at Coney Island amusement park in Brooklyn, New York. This was the first North American roller coaster. It had a speed of 6 miles (10 kilometers) per hour.

In the early 1900s, people started building larger and faster wooden coasters. An engineer named John Miller added upstop wheels to cars. These wheels run underneath rails. Upstop wheels help keep cars on the rails. They make coasters safer to operate at high speeds. After the addition of upstop wheels, coasters could travel at speeds of about 50 miles (80 kilometers) per hour. They also could make sharper turns.

During the 1920s, amusement park owners built many large wooden coasters in the United States. This time was called the "Golden Age of Roller Coasters." In 1927, a wooden coaster named Cyclone opened at Coney Island amusement park. This ride quickly became popular. The Cyclone has an 85-foot (26-meter) drop. Cars reach speeds of 55 miles (89 kilometers) per hour.

The Golden Age ended when the United States entered the Great Depression (1929–1939). Millions of people lost their jobs during this time. They no longer could afford to spend money at amusement parks. Many amusement parks closed and were torn down during the Great Depression.

New amusement parks were built after the Great Depression. In 1955, Disneyland opened in Anaheim, California. This theme park quickly became one of the most popular amusement parks in the United States. Theme parks have rides and structures that are based on a certain subject. Many other new theme

**The Cyclone became a popular coaster during the Golden Age of Roller Coasters.**

parks then opened. These parks often had a roller coaster as a main attraction.

The new parks helped roller coasters become popular again in the 1960s. The Beast opened in 1979 and attracted many people to Kings Island.

## Riding The Beast

The Beast has many features. The ride starts with a lift hill that is 135 feet (41 meters) high. The cars pass by trees as they travel down this hill. The track then enters a tunnel. Part of this tunnel is underground.

The Beast has two other tunnels that are above ground. The first tunnel is 235 feet (72 meters) long. Cars come out of this tunnel and climb a hill. The cars reach their fastest speed at the bottom of the hill and then enter the last tunnel. This tunnel covers a helix. This curve changes in elevation. The track makes one large circle and part of another circle to form the helix. The entire curve is more than 600 feet (180 meters) long. Brakes then slow down the cars as the ride ends.

**Tunnels cover part of The Beast's track.**

# Chapter 3

# The Big One

The Big One is a hypercoaster located at Blackpool Pleasure Beach. This amusement park is in Blackpool, England. The Big One was the world's tallest coaster when it opened in 1994. Its height is 214 feet (65 meters). The Big One still is Europe's tallest coaster.

## History of Hypercoasters

Roller coaster manufacturers have been building steel coasters like The Big One for about 40 years. In 1959, a company called Arrow Dynamics built the world's first steel coaster. This bobsled coaster is called the Matterhorn. It is located at Disneyland. Roller coaster manufacturers built many steel coasters in the early 1970s. These coasters were popular because

**The Big One is the tallest roller coaster in Europe.**

they had inversions. In 1989, Arrow Dynamics built the first hypercoaster. This coaster is the Magnum XL 200. Arrow Dynamics soon became known for building hypercoasters.

The Big One's design is based on the Magnum XL 200. Workers spent two years building The Big One.

## Riding The Big One

The Big One is located near the Irish Sea. This sea borders England's northwestern coast. Riders can view the Irish Sea from the top of the lift hill.

Cars begin traveling up the lift hill inside a large model of a soda pop can. The Big One's lift hill has a 65-degree drop. The cars reach a speed of 76 miles (122 kilometers) per hour in just 3 seconds during this drop.

The cars then travel over track that includes many features. They go over a second hill. They then curve around a large circle. The track goes over and around other rides in the

**The Big One's lift hill has a 65-degree drop.**

amusement park. The cars later go around
a helix.

The cars enter a tunnel near the ride's end.
The tunnel's roof seems too low for the cars to
enter. But the cars move through the tunnel
safely. The cars then make a few sharp turns
before they enter the station.

# Chapter 4

# Volcano, The Blast Coaster

Volcano, The Blast Coaster is an inverted steel roller coaster at Paramount's Kings Dominion. This amusement park is located in Doswell, Virginia. Volcano is the world's fastest inverted coaster. Its top speed is 70 miles (113 kilometers) per hour.

Volcano has other special features. The station is inside a large model of a volcano. Volcano's track goes through and around the outside of this model.

Volcano is the world's first inverted coaster to use a linear induction motor (LIM) for power. Most other roller coasters use gravity to power cars. The cars gain enough speed as they

Fire sometimes shoots out of the volcano's top.

descend the lift hill to keep the cars moving throughout the circuit. The LIM is located in the tracks. It uses electricity to create a magnetic force. This force attracts metal. The coaster's cars have metal fins on their sides. These wide, flat fins are made of a strong, lightweight metal called aluminum. The fins are located between the cars' wheels and the seats. The magnetic force attracts the aluminum fins and pulls the cars along the track.

## Inversions and Inverted Coasters

Engineers first made wooden coasters with inversions in the late 1800s. Cars on these coasters usually traveled down a steep hill and around a loop. But rides over these inversions often were rough. Riders sometimes suffered back and neck injuries. Engineers later made steel coasters with inversions that were smoother for riders. The first steel coaster with inversions was built in 1975. This coaster was the Corkscrew at Knott's Berry Farm in Buena Park, California.

**Riders of Volcano, The Blast Coaster travel on four inversions.**

In 1992, a Swiss roller coaster company called B&M designed the first inverted coaster. This coaster is called Batman: The Ride. It is located at Six Flags Great America in Gurnee, Illinois. Many amusement park owners later hired companies to build inverted coasters. Five more inverted Batman coasters are located at Six Flag amusement parks in the United States. Other inverted coasters include The

The cars reach a height of 155 feet (47 meters) at the top of the volcano.

Great Bear at Hersheypark, Pennsylvania, and Top Gun at Paramount Canada's Wonderland. This amusement park is in Vaughn, Ontario, Canada.

### Riding Volcano

Riders on Volcano first travel through a tunnel inside the volcano model. The cars travel as fast as 70 miles (113 kilometers) per hour through this tunnel. The cars then exit the volcano and turn to the left. The cars soon re-enter the volcano. The track is nearly at a 90-degree angle at this time. Power from the LIM pushes the cars upward. The cars come out of the volcano's top. The cars are 155 feet (47 meters) above the ground at this point.

Riders next encounter a variety of features. The cars make four inversions. Sharp turns are located between these inversions. The track curves around the outside of the volcano and passes under and around waterfalls. Volcano, The Blast Coaster ends with an 80-foot (24-meter) drop. Brakes slow down the cars as they enter the station.

# Chapter 5

# Superman: The Escape

Superman: The Escape is a steel shuttle coaster located at Six Flags Magic Mountain. This amusement park is in Valencia, California. Superman: The Escape is the world's fastest and tallest roller coaster. Superman has a top speed of 100 miles (161 kilometers) per hour. It is 415 feet (126 meters) high. The coaster is as tall as a 41-story building.

Superman has two side-by-side tracks. Only one car rides on each track. Each of these cars weighs 6 tons (5.4 metric tons) and has four large wheels. The wheels are about 2 feet (.6 meter) tall. Each car carries 15 people.

Most roller coasters have a lift hill. But Superman's cars start traveling on a long, flat

**Superman: The Escape is the world's tallest coaster.**

track. Motors push the cars along this track at high speeds. The cars then go up a tower at the end of the track. The cars reach a speed of 100 miles (161 kilometers) per hour as they fall back down the tower. This part of the ride is called a freefall. The motors do not operate during the freefall. The entire ride lasts about 30 seconds.

## Magnet Power

Superman: The Escape uses special motors to power its cars. These motors are called linear synchronous motors (LSMs). LSMs are similar to Volcano, The Blast Coaster's LIM. Both types of motors use electricity to create magnetism. But Superman's motors use magnetism differently than an LIM motor uses it. LSMs follow a law of magnetism. This law states that the like ends of two magnets push away from each other. It also states that the unlike ends of two magnets attract each other.

A series of LSMs line Superman's tracks. Large magnets are on the bottom of the cars. The LSMs operate one after another. One end of an LSM attracts a car's magnet. This pulls the

**LSMs push Superman's cars along the tracks.**

car forward. The car then passes over the LSM. The other end of the LSM then pushes the car's magnet away. The car then moves to the next LSM. This process allows Superman's cars to reach a high speed in a short amount of time.

## Building Superman
Roller coaster engineers started planning Superman: The Escape in 1994. They tested

their plans on a computer to make sure the ride would operate properly and safely.

Engineers first tested Superman in 1996. But Superman did not run at the expected speed. It only ran at about 94 miles (150 kilometers) per hour. Engineers then made changes to computers that control the LSMs. These motors need to turn on and off at the proper times. Engineers also added a new power line to supply electricity to Superman's LSMs. Superman: The Escape opened in 1997.

## Riding Superman

Riders of Superman: The Escape start their trip at a station located inside of an ice cave model. This cave is a model of Superman's Fortress of Solitude. Superman sometimes lived in this cave. Doors in the cave open to let the riders enter a car.

The ride begins as the car shoots along the track. It reaches a speed of 100 miles (161 kilometers) per hour in just 7 seconds. The car then travels up a tower. This tower has a 90-degree slope. The car then falls backward

**Riders of Superman begin their journey in an ice cave model.**

down the tower. Riders feel as if they are weightless for 6 seconds. This feeling also is called airtime. Riders often feel as if they will come out of their seats during airtime. No other roller coaster matches this length of airtime. After the backward fall, the car soon arrives back at the ice cave.

# FAST FACTS

## THE BEAST

Type: Wooden out-and-back/twister
Location: Paramount's Kings Island,
Kings Island, Ohio
Top Speed: 64 miles (103
kilometers) per hour
Height: 135 feet (41 meters)
Length: 7,400 feet (2,256 meters)
Maximum G Force: 4.5
Opened: 1979

## THE BIG ONE

Type: Steel hypercoaster
Location: Blackpool Pleasure Beach,
Blackpool, England
Top Speed: 76 miles (122
kilometers) per hour
Height: 214 feet (65 meters)
Length: 5,497 feet (1,675 meters)
Maximum G Force: 3.6
Opened: 1994

## VOLCANO, THE BLAST COASTER

Type: Steel inverted coaster
Location: Paramount's Kings Dominion, Doswell, Virginia
Top Speed: 70 miles (113 kilometers) per hour
Height: 155 feet (47 meters)
Length: 2,757 feet (840 meters)
Maximum G Force: 5
Opened: 1998

## SUPERMAN: THE ESCAPE

Type: Steel shuttle coaster
Location: Six Flags Magic Mountain, Valencia, California
Top Speed: 100 miles (161 kilometers) per hour
Height: 415 feet (126 meters)
Length: 1,315 feet (401 meters)
Maximum G Force: 4.5
Opened: 1997

# Chapter 6

# The Future of Roller Coasters

Roller coasters are among the most popular rides in the world. Amusement parks add new coasters every year. North American amusement parks sometimes open more than 50 new roller coasters in one year.

## Design Improvements

Roller coaster engineers often improve roller coasters. In the future, they may try to break speed and height records. They may design new track layouts. Engineers also may create more looping wooden coasters. Today, Son of Beast is the world's only looping wooden coaster.

---

**Son of Beast is the world's fastest, tallest, and only looping wooden coaster.**

Engineers also may create new ways for people to ride coasters. In 2000, Paramount's Great America in Santa Clara, California, opened Stealth. The seats on this roller coaster tilt. Riders spend most of their time lying on their backs or stomachs. This is the first coaster on which riders lie down.

## Roller Coaster Prototypes

Roller coaster engineers sometimes build new types of roller coasters. These coasters are called prototypes. In 1990, Arrow Dynamics built a coaster on which the cars ride between two tracks. This coaster is called the Pipeline. The Pipeline is the first coaster to perform barrel rolls. Cars travel sideways in a complete circle on these inversions. Today, six coasters can perform barrel rolls. One of these coasters is Ultra Twister at Six Flags AstroWorld in Houston, Texas. Five more of these coasters are located in Japan. A few coasters have similar inversions called heartline flips.

Another roller coaster prototype is Thrust Air 2000. A company from Utah called S&S Power designed this prototype. It uses air power to

**Engineers will continue to build many new roller coasters in the future.**

move cars up a 90-degree hill. The cars reach a speed of 80 miles (129 kilometers) per hour in less than 2 seconds. Thrust Air 2000 may open to the public in the future.

People who ride roller coasters are adventurous. They enjoy the thrill when the cars make sharp turns and inversions. Roller coaster engineers continue to work to make faster, taller, and more exciting roller coasters.

# Words to Know

**barrel roll** (BA-ruhl ROLL)—a type of inversion in which cars turn in a circle sideways

**circuit** (SUR-kit)—a roller coaster's entire track

**corkscrew** (KORK-skroo)—a section of a roller coaster's track that twists into a spiral; corkscrews are one type of inversion.

**gravity** (GRAV-uh-tee)—the force that pulls objects down toward Earth's surface

**helix** (HEE-liks)—a curve that changes in elevation

**hypercoaster** (hye-pur-KOHSS-tur)—a roller coaster that is more than 200 feet (60 meters) high

**inversion** (in-VUR-shuhn)—a section of a roller coaster's track that turns riders upside down

# To Learn More

**Alter, Judy.** *Amusement Parks: Roller Coasters, Ferris Wheels, and Cotton Candy.* A First Book. New York: Franklin Watts, 1997.

**Chandler, Gil.** *Roller Coasters.* Cruisin'. Mankato, Minn.: Capstone Books, 1995.

**Cook, Nick.** *Roller Coasters, or, I Had So Much Fun, I Almost Puked.* Minneapolis: Carolrhoda Books, 1998.

**Schafer, Mike and Scott Rutherford.** *Roller Coasters.* Enthusiast Color. Osceola, Wis.: MBI Publishing, 1998.

**Throgmorton, Todd H.** *Roller Coasters: United States and Canada.* Jefferson, N.C.: McFarland, 2000.

# Useful Addresses

**American Coaster Enthusiasts**
5800 Foxridge Drive
Suite 115
Mission, KS  66202-2333

**Coaster Enthusiasts of Canada**
23 Sheridan Street
Dartmouth, NS  B3A 2C9
Canada

**International Association of Amusement
  Parks and Attractions**
1448 Duke Street
Alexandria, VA  22314

# Internet Sites

Visit the FactHound at *www.facthound.com*

All the FactHound sites are hand-selected by our editors. FactHound will fetch the best, most accurate information to answer your questions.

IT'S EASY! IT'S FUN!
1) Go to *www.facthound.com*
2) Type in: **0736805710**
3) Click on **FETCH IT** and FactHound will put you on the trail of several helpful links.

You can also search by subject or book title. So, relax and let our pal FactHound do the research for you!

# Index